MADEIRA WINTER ESCAPE TRAVEL GUIDE

2026

Your Levada Walks, Whale Watching, Cozy Towns & Off-Season Savings.

Amy Lester

Copyright © [Amy Lester], 2026

All rights reserved. No part of this book may be reproduced, stored in a retrieval system, or transmitted in any form or by any means—electronic, mechanical, photocopying, recording, or otherwise—without prior written permission of the publisher, except in the case of brief quotations embodied in reviews or articles.
This book is a work of nonfiction. While the author has made every effort to provide accurate and up-to-date information at the time of publication, they accept no liability for any errors, omissions, or changes in details. Travelers are advised to verify information before planning their trips.

Contents

Dedication

Acknowledgments

Preface

Chapter 1: Welcome to Madeira — The Island of Eternal Spring

Chapter 2: Why Visit Madeira in Winter

Chapter 3: Planning Your Winter Escape

Chapter 4: Where to Stay — Cozy Retreats to Oceanfront Luxury

Chapter 5: Getting Around Madeira

Chapter 6: Winter Experiences You Can't Miss

Chapter 7: Exploring Funchal and Beyond

Chapter 8: Food, Wine, and Local Flavors

Chapter 9: Madeira for Every Type of Traveler

Chapter 10: Suggested Winter Itineraries

Bonus Chapter: Hidden Madeira — Local Secrets & Underrated Experiences

Conclusion: Leaving Madeira, Carrying the Warmth With You

Appendix

Dedication

This book is for the winter wanderers who refuse to hibernate, for the sun-seekers who understand that warmth is not only a matter of temperature, and for the travelers who deliberately choose stillness and beauty when much of the world retreats indoors. I wrote these pages with you in mind—the curious, the contemplative, and the quietly adventurous.

I still remember the first winter I escaped to Madeira. While friends back home were layering coats and counting down grey days, I was standing on a cliff above the Atlantic, watching clouds drift lazily over volcanic peaks. The air was cool but gentle, scented with salt and eucalyptus. It felt like discovering a secret: an island where winter softens instead of hardens, where life continues outdoors at an unhurried pace. That feeling—of stepping out of the cold and into calm—is what inspired this guide.

This dedication is also for those who travel not to tick boxes, but to feel present. Madeira rewards that kind of traveler. It invites you to walk slowly along levada paths, to linger over long lunches, to sit quietly at viewpoints where the ocean seems endless. In winter especially, the island reveals a more intimate version of itself—fewer crowds, clearer light, and a deeper connection with local life.

To help you visualize and plan your own escape, here are a few practical notes drawn from experience and research, woven into the spirit of this dedication:

Suggested Travel Dates

Late November through early March is my favorite window for a winter visit. December offers festive lights and Christmas markets, January brings peaceful landscapes and excellent hiking weather, and February to early March is ideal for whale watching along the coast.

Average Daily Costs (Winter Estimates)

- Mid-range accommodation: €80–€130 per night
- Local meals and cafés: €15–€25 per day
- Car rental: €30–€45 per day
- Guided experiences or tours: €40–€70 per activity

Winter often comes with better value for money, making it easier to stay longer and travel more thoughtfully.

Unique Photo Opportunities

- Sunrise above the clouds in Pico do Arieiro

- Misty levada walks framed by laurel forests

- Golden-hour views over Funchal harbor from Monte

- Winter seas crashing against the natural pools of Porto Moniz

These are not staged moments; they are quiet, honest scenes that Madeira offers freely to those who slow down enough to notice.

I dedicate this book to your decision to travel differently—to seek light when days are short, to embrace calm instead of chaos, and to trust that some of the most meaningful journeys happen when the world seems to be standing still. May Madeira meet you with warmth, and may you leave carrying a little of its peace with you, long after winter has passed.

Acknowledgments

To the People of Madeira

This guide would not exist without the generosity of the Madeiran people, whose warmth defines the island as much as its climate. From café owners who patiently explained the difference between local wines, to taxi drivers who doubled as informal historians, every conversation added texture to my understanding of the island. During my winter stay, locals were especially open—perhaps because the pace slows and there is time to talk. I was invited into kitchens, guided along lesser-known walking paths, and offered advice that never appears on brochures. Those moments shaped the practical insight woven throughout this book.

- **Suggested Travel Dates:** December to February, when daily life is most visible and unhurried

- **Average Daily Costs:** €20–€30 for meals at local eateries

- **Unique Photo Opportunities:** Early morning scenes at neighborhood cafés, fishermen preparing boats in Câmara de Lobos, quiet streets in Funchal before shops open

Fellow Travelers Who Shared the Road

I am grateful to the travelers I met along levada paths, mountain viewpoints, and ferry docks—people who shared stories over coffee or exchanged recommendations mid-hike. In winter, the island attracts a particular kind of visitor: reflective, curious, and often traveling alone or in small groups. These conversations confirmed that Madeira is not only a destination but a shared experience. Tips about trail conditions, hidden viewpoints, and weather patterns often came from strangers who became temporary companions.

- **Suggested Travel Dates:** January for hiking conversations and scenic viewpoints

- **Average Daily Costs:** €10–€15 for shared coffee stops or bakery visits

- **Unique Photo Opportunities:** Candid trail moments, silhouettes at mountain viewpoints, ferry decks framed by winter skies

Storytellers, Writers, and Quiet Researchers

This book also stands on the shoulders of historians, winemakers, botanists, and local writers who have documented Madeira long before I arrived. Museums, archives, and small exhibitions filled in the gaps between experience and understanding. I spent rainy afternoons reading about volcanic formations and maritime trade, then stepped outside to see those stories reflected in stone streets and terraced hillsides. Research did not feel academic here—it felt alive and grounded.

- **Suggested Travel Dates:** Rainier winter days in December and January
- **Average Daily Costs:** €5–€10 for museum entries and local publications
- **Unique Photo Opportunities:** Historic interiors, handwritten menus, wine cellars with aging barrels

The Landscapes That Spoke Without Words

Some acknowledgments belong to places rather than people. The laurel forests in winter mist, the Atlantic during a January swell, and the silence of high-altitude viewpoints at dawn all left lasting impressions. These landscapes provided clarity and perspective, often in moments when no conversation was needed. Walking alone along a levada in winter teaches patience and presence; it is a lesson that shaped how I wrote every chapter.

- **Suggested Travel Dates:** November to March for dramatic weather and changing light

- **Average Daily Costs:** Free for self-guided walks; €40–€60 for guided hikes

- **Unique Photo Opportunities:** Fog rolling through forests, sunlight breaking over cliffs, long-exposure ocean shots

The Quiet Moments In Between

Finally, I acknowledge the unplanned pauses—the afternoons spent watching rain trace patterns on café windows, the evenings listening to distant waves from a hotel balcony, the slow mornings with no agenda. These moments taught me how Madeira reveals itself best when you stop trying to conquer it. This guide is shaped as much by stillness as by movement.

- **Suggested Travel Dates:** Midweek winter days for uninterrupted calm

- **Average Daily Costs:** €0–€10 for coffee and reflection time

- **Unique Photo Opportunities:** Window reflections, empty viewpoints, twilight harbor scenes

This book is a collective effort, even if written in a single voice. Every recommendation, observation, and detail carries the imprint of those who shared their island, their time, and their stories with me. I offer my sincere gratitude to all of them—and to you, the reader, for choosing to travel with intention.

Preface

Why I Chose Madeira When Winter Closed In

I did not come to Madeira to escape winter entirely, but to soften it. My search was for a place where I could still walk outdoors without bracing against the cold, where nature remained alive, and where days unfolded at a humane pace. Madeira met those needs quietly and confidently. The island does not shout for attention; it reveals itself gradually, especially in winter. With daytime temperatures that hover comfortably between cool and warm, I found myself hiking, sitting by the sea, and exploring towns without the pressure of summer crowds.

Winter in Madeira feels intentional rather than accidental. The light is gentle, the landscapes dramatic, and the atmosphere reflective. Instead of rushing between attractions, I learned to move with the rhythm of the island—slow mornings, long walks, unhurried meals. That rhythm is what convinced me that Madeira is not simply a destination, but an experience worth understanding deeply.

- **Suggested Travel Dates:** Late November to early March

- **Average Daily Costs:** €90–€140 including accommodation, meals, and local transport

- **Unique Photo Opportunities:** Soft winter sunlight over terraced hillsides, cloud inversions in the mountains, empty coastal promenades

What Makes Madeira a True Winter Escape

Madeira's appeal in winter lies in its balance. The island offers warmth without excess, beauty without spectacle, and adventure without chaos. I could hike along levada paths in the morning, enjoy a leisurely lunch in Funchal, and watch the sunset over the Atlantic—all in one day, without rushing. The absence of mass tourism during winter allows for genuine interactions with locals and a deeper connection to place.

From a practical standpoint, winter travel here is also sensible. Flights are often more affordable, accommodation is easier to secure, and popular attractions feel accessible rather than overwhelming. Even activities like whale watching and wine tasting feel more personal during this season. Madeira does not shut down in winter; it simply exhales.

- **Suggested Travel Dates:** January for calm and clarity, February for wildlife experiences
- **Average Daily Costs:** €25–€40 for meals, €30–€50 for activities

- **Unique Photo Opportunities:** Whale sightings offshore, vineyard slopes in winter light, harbor reflections after rain

Beyond Postcards: Experiencing the Real Island

It is easy to fall in love with Madeira's famous viewpoints and dramatic coastlines, but the island's soul reveals itself elsewhere. I discovered it in neighborhood bakeries, on quiet side streets, and along lesser-known walking paths where the only sounds were wind and water. Winter is the ideal time for this kind of exploration. Without the noise of peak season, the island feels approachable and sincere.

This guide is designed to take you beyond the familiar images. I focus on experiences that encourage observation rather than consumption—where to linger, when to walk, and how to notice small details that define daily life. These are not secrets guarded by locals, but moments overlooked by hurried visitors.

- **Suggested Travel Dates:** December and January for slower local rhythms
- **Average Daily Costs:** €10–€20 for cafés, local bakeries, and markets
- **Unique Photo Opportunities:** Street-level details, market produce, quiet village squares

How This Guide Is Meant to Be Used

I wrote this book as a companion, not a checklist. You can follow the itineraries closely or use them as loose frameworks, adapting them to your pace and interests. Each chapter builds on lived experience combined with careful research, offering context as well as practical advice. I explain not only what to do, but why certain choices matter—where staying longer enhances the experience, and when moving on makes sense.

You will find suggested travel dates, cost estimates, and photographic highlights throughout the book, not as rigid instructions but as tools to help you plan with confidence. My goal is to remove uncertainty so you can focus on presence.

- **Suggested Travel Dates:** Flexible across winter months
- **Average Daily Costs:** Adjustable based on travel style
- **Unique Photo Opportunities:** Personal moments—morning light, shared meals, unplanned discoveries

An Invitation to Travel Differently

Madeira taught me that winter travel does not have to be about escape alone; it can be about reconnection. This guide invites you to approach the island with curiosity, patience, and respect for its natural and cultural rhythms. If you allow yourself to slow down, Madeira will meet you halfway, offering warmth that lingers beyond the season.

As you turn the page, consider this book an open invitation—to step off familiar routes, to stay present, and to experience Madeira not as a backdrop, but as a living, breathing place that rewards attention.

Chapter 1: Welcome to Madeira — The Island of Eternal Spring

First Impressions of an Atlantic Island

My first encounter with Madeira felt less like arriving somewhere new and more like being gently welcomed. As the plane descended over the Atlantic, the island emerged dramatically from the ocean—steep cliffs, deep valleys, and terraced hillsides layered with green. Madeira is a Portuguese archipelago situated off the northwest coast of Africa, closer to Morocco than mainland Portugal, yet unmistakably European in rhythm and order. That geographical position explains much of its magic: ocean-moderated weather, fertile volcanic soil, and landscapes that shift quickly from sea level to mountain peaks.

Winter was the season that allowed me to absorb these contrasts without distraction. The air felt crisp but kind, and visibility was often sharper than in summer. Even on my first day, I noticed how the island invites observation rather than urgency. You arrive, you look, and slowly, you understand.

- **Suggested Travel Dates:** November to March

- **Average Daily Costs:** €90–€150 including accommodation and meals

- **Unique Photo Opportunities:** Aerial coastal views, terraced hillsides seen from winding roads, harbor panoramas on arrival

Madeira's Geography: Small Island, Vast Variety

Madeira may appear compact on a map, but its terrain is anything but simple. Volcanic origins have carved the island into dramatic ridges, fertile valleys, and abrupt coastal cliffs. In a single winter day, I could walk along the shoreline in the morning and stand above the clouds by afternoon. The island's highest peaks—Pico do Arieiro and Pico Ruivo—often collect mist in winter, creating an almost surreal atmosphere that feels worlds away from the coast below.

The famous levadas—irrigation channels built centuries ago—trace the island's contours and make its interior accessible. Walking these paths in winter was especially rewarding: water flowed steadily, vegetation was lush, and temperatures were ideal for long hikes. Madeira's geography does not demand endurance so much as attention. Every turn reveals a new perspective.

- **Suggested Travel Dates:** December to February for hiking and mountain views

- **Average Daily Costs:** €0 for self-guided walks; €45–€65 for guided hikes

- **Unique Photo Opportunities:** Cloud inversions, forested levada paths, cliffside viewpoints

A Culture Shaped by the Sea and the Land

Madeiran culture is deeply rooted in self-reliance and hospitality, shaped by centuries of isolation and maritime trade. I felt this most clearly in everyday interactions—quiet efficiency paired with genuine warmth. The island's connection to the sea remains strong, evident in its cuisine, festivals, and daily routines. Fishing villages like Câmara de Lobos still move at a pace dictated by tides rather than timetables.

Winter revealed the cultural fabric more clearly. Without the intensity of peak tourism, I was able to observe local life as it unfolds naturally. Markets felt communal rather than performative, and conversations flowed easily. Madeira's culture does not try to impress; it simply continues, inviting visitors to join respectfully.

- **Suggested Travel Dates:** January for authentic local rhythms

- **Average Daily Costs:** €15–€30 for traditional meals and markets

- **Unique Photo Opportunities:** Harbor activity, local markets, village streets at dusk

A Brief History That Still Shapes the Island

Madeira's history is inseparable from exploration. Discovered by Portuguese navigators in the 15th century, the island quickly became a strategic Atlantic outpost. Sugar production brought early prosperity, followed by wine, which secured Madeira's place in global trade routes. Walking through Funchal, I could still trace these layers—fortifications near the harbor, elegant wine lodges, and colonial-era architecture adapted to modern life.

Winter offered the time and space to engage with this history thoughtfully. Museums were quiet, historical sites unrushed. The island's past feels present here, not frozen behind glass but integrated into daily living. Understanding this context deepened every experience, from tasting wine to walking old streets.

- **Suggested Travel Dates:** December to February for museum visits

- **Average Daily Costs:** €5–€12 for historical sites and museums

- **Unique Photo Opportunities:** Stone architecture, wine cellars, historic harbor views

Why Winter Is Madeira's Best-Kept Secret

What truly distinguishes Madeira in winter is balance. The climate remains mild, typically ranging from cool mornings to comfortable afternoons, making outdoor exploration effortless. Unlike many winter destinations, the island does not feel dormant. Instead, it feels focused. Trails are quieter, restaurants more attentive, and nature more expressive.

Personally, winter allowed me to experience Madeira without compromise. I hiked, explored, photographed, and rested—all without contending with crowds or heat. It is a season that rewards curiosity and patience, offering a more intimate version of the island.

- **Suggested Travel Dates:** Late November through early March
- **Average Daily Costs:** €80–€130 due to off-season pricing
- **Unique Photo Opportunities:** Empty viewpoints, winter seas, soft golden light over the Atlantic

Understanding Madeira Before You Explore

Before diving into itineraries and recommendations, it helps to understand what Madeira offers at its core. This is an island defined by contrasts—between land and sea, past and present, movement and stillness. Winter strips away excess and reveals essence. My hope is that by understanding Madeira's geography, culture, and history from the outset, you will explore with greater awareness and appreciation.

As you continue through this guide, consider this chapter your foundation. Madeira is not a place to rush through; it is a place to arrive slowly, especially in winter, when the island shows its truest self.

Chapter 2: Why Visit Madeira in Winter

A Climate That Redefines Winter

Winter in Madeira does not resemble winter as most travelers know it. When I arrived in January, I was met with soft sunlight, fresh ocean air, and temperatures that made walking outdoors a pleasure rather than a challenge. Days were comfortably mild, while evenings carried just enough coolness to invite a light jacket. This is the advantage of Madeira's Atlantic location: the ocean moderates extremes, creating a climate that feels stable and forgiving.

What stood out most was how usable the weather felt. I could hike for hours without overheating, sit outdoors at cafés, and explore towns without rushing indoors. Occasional rain refreshed the landscape rather than disrupting plans. Winter here is not about escaping cold entirely; it is about inhabiting a season that encourages movement and presence.

- **Suggested Travel Dates:** December to February for the most consistent winter conditions

- **Average Daily Costs:** €90–€140

- **Unique Photo Opportunities:** Clear mountain vistas after rain, winter light over the coastline, dramatic cloud formations

Fewer Crowds, Deeper Experiences

One of the most compelling reasons I recommend Madeira in winter is the absence of crowds. Popular viewpoints, levada walks, and coastal promenades felt accessible and personal. I was able to stop, observe, and photograph without navigating around tour groups or competing for space. This shift changes the entire travel experience.

In winter, interactions feel more genuine. Restaurant owners have time to talk, guides tailor their explanations, and locals move through their routines unhurried. I found myself learning more simply because there was space to ask questions and listen. Madeira becomes less of a spectacle and more of a conversation.

- **Suggested Travel Dates:** January for maximum quiet

- **Average Daily Costs:** €20–€35 for meals in less touristy areas

- **Unique Photo Opportunities:** Empty viewpoints, uninterrupted coastal walks, candid street scenes

Better Value Without Compromise

Traveling in winter also made financial sense. Accommodation prices were noticeably lower, and availability was rarely an issue. I stayed in well-located hotels and apartments that would be far more expensive during summer months. Car rentals, tours, and even flights often came at reduced rates, allowing me to allocate my budget toward experiences rather than logistics.

Importantly, lower costs did not translate to limited offerings. Restaurants, attractions, and transport operated normally. The island remains fully functional in winter, simply less pressured. For travelers who value quality and flexibility, this season offers a rare balance.

- **Suggested Travel Dates:** Late November to early March for best pricing

- **Average Daily Costs:** €80–€120 depending on accommodation choice

- **Unique Photo Opportunities:** Hotel balconies with unobstructed views, quiet marinas, sunrise over empty roads

Seasonal Highlights You Can Only Experience in Winter

Winter reveals aspects of Madeira that summer cannot. The mountains often collect mist, creating ethereal landscapes that shift throughout the day. Levada paths are at their greenest, fed by seasonal rainfall. The ocean, more dramatic in winter, adds energy to coastal scenery and makes places like Porto Moniz especially striking.

Wildlife experiences also peak during this season. Whale and dolphin sightings are common, and winter seas create ideal conditions for observation. These moments—watching marine life surface against a grey-blue horizon—remain some of my most vivid memories of the island.

- **Suggested Travel Dates:** February for whale watching and lush landscapes

- **Average Daily Costs:** €45–€70 for guided wildlife tours

- **Unique Photo Opportunities:** Breaching whales, misty forests, waves crashing against volcanic pools

Festivals That Add Warmth to the Season

Winter in Madeira is far from quiet culturally. December brings Christmas celebrations marked by lights, markets, and traditional music. I was surprised by how vibrant Funchal felt during this time—festive but not overwhelming. Local traditions take center stage, and celebrations feel community-driven rather than commercial.

As winter transitions toward spring, preparations for Carnival begin, filling towns with color and anticipation. These events provide insight into Madeiran identity and offer travelers a chance to participate rather than simply observe. Timing a visit around these festivals adds texture to the experience.

- **Suggested Travel Dates:** December for Christmas festivities; February for Carnival season

- **Average Daily Costs:** €10–€20 for markets and local events

- **Unique Photo Opportunities:** Illuminated streets, traditional costumes, evening celebrations

The Subtle Magic of Traveling Slower

What ultimately makes winter travel in Madeira special is the pace it encourages. Without heat or crowds dictating movement, I found myself traveling more intuitively. Mornings unfolded slowly, plans remained flexible, and unexpected moments often became highlights. Winter allowed Madeira to feel less like a destination and more like a temporary home.

This slower rhythm invites reflection. You notice changes in light, conversations last longer, and experiences deepen. Madeira in winter rewards those willing to pause, observe, and engage with the island on its own terms.

- **Suggested Travel Dates:** January and early February for the most relaxed atmosphere

- **Average Daily Costs:** €0–€15 for unplanned cafés and spontaneous stops

- **Unique Photo Opportunities:** Twilight over Funchal, quiet harbor scenes, reflective moments along levadas

Why Winter Reveals the Island's True Character

Winter strips Madeira down to its essentials—land, sea, culture, and community. Without distraction, the island's character becomes clearer and more generous. My time here during the colder months reshaped how I think about winter travel entirely. Madeira does not simply offer an alternative to cold destinations; it offers a more thoughtful way to experience a place.

For travelers seeking warmth, value, authenticity, and space to breathe, winter is not a compromise—it is Madeira at its best.

Chapter 3: Planning Your Winter Escape

Getting to Madeira: Flights and Entry Requirements

Planning a winter escape to Madeira begins with understanding how to reach the island smoothly. I flew into Cristiano Ronaldo Madeira International Airport in Funchal, which is the main gateway and well-connected to major European cities, particularly during winter when airlines increase routes for seasonal travelers. Direct flights are common from Portugal, the UK, Germany, and other parts of Europe, while travelers from outside Europe typically connect through Lisbon.

For most visitors, entry is straightforward. Madeira is part of Portugal and the Schengen Area, so visa requirements mirror those of mainland Portugal. During my preparation, I found it helpful to check entry rules early, especially for passport validity and length-of-stay limits. Winter travel often comes with fewer crowds at immigration, making arrival noticeably calm.

- **Suggested Travel Dates:** Late November to March for flexible flight options

- **Average Flight Costs:** €120–€250 from Europe; €450–€750 from outside Europe

- **Unique Photo Opportunities:** Aerial approach over cliffs, runway views meeting the Atlantic, first harbor glimpse from the plane

What to Pack for a Madeiran Winter

Packing for Madeira in winter requires balance rather than bulk. I learned quickly that heavy winter coats are unnecessary, but layers are essential. Mornings in the mountains can be cool, while afternoons along the coast feel pleasantly warm. A light jacket, breathable sweaters, and comfortable walking shoes covered most situations.

Hiking gear was especially useful. Waterproof footwear, a compact rain jacket, and a small daypack allowed me to explore levadas and coastal trails comfortably. I also packed swimwear—natural pools and hotel spas remain inviting year-round. Thoughtful packing made movement effortless and eliminated the need for constant adjustments.

- **Suggested Travel Dates:** December to February for layered packing

- **Average Packing Costs:** €0–€50 depending on existing gear

- **Unique Photo Opportunities:** Layered outfits against dramatic landscapes, winter hikes framed by lush greenery

Travel Insurance and Health Preparation

Travel insurance is one area I never compromise on, especially for winter travel. Madeira's terrain is beautiful but rugged, and activities like hiking and whale watching carry inherent risks. I chose a policy that covered medical care, trip interruptions, and outdoor activities. This decision paid off in peace of mind, allowing me to explore confidently.

Healthcare on the island is reliable, and pharmacies are widely available. European travelers can use their health insurance cards, while others should ensure coverage includes emergency treatment. Preparing these details in advance made my trip feel organized and stress-free.

- **Suggested Travel Dates:** All winter months

- **Average Insurance Costs:** €20–€60 for short stays
- **Unique Photo Opportunities:** Not applicable, but peace of mind enhances every experience

Managing Money: Currency and Payments

Madeira uses the euro, and financial logistics were refreshingly simple. ATMs are widely available, and card payments are accepted in most hotels, restaurants, and shops. That said, I found carrying some cash useful for small cafés, markets, and rural areas. Winter made transactions easier, with shorter lines and more attentive service.

Budgeting felt manageable. Prices in winter were consistent and predictable, and I rarely encountered unexpected expenses. Setting a daily spending range helped me enjoy meals and experiences without constant calculation.

- **Suggested Travel Dates:** Winter off-season for consistent pricing

- **Average Daily Spend:** €30–€50 excluding accommodation

- **Unique Photo Opportunities:** Market stalls, café counters, wine tastings

Staying Safe and Traveling Responsibly

Madeira felt remarkably safe, even when walking alone in the evenings. Crime rates are low, and locals are accustomed to visitors. Still, basic awareness matters. I paid attention to weather updates, particularly for mountain hikes where conditions can change quickly in winter. Informing someone of hiking plans and respecting trail closures ensured safety without limiting exploration.

Driving requires extra caution. Winter roads in mountainous areas can be narrow and foggy. Renting a car with good traction and avoiding night driving in unfamiliar areas made a significant difference. These small decisions shaped a smoother experience.

- **Suggested Travel Dates:** January and February for quieter roads

- **Average Safety Costs:** €30–€50 for car upgrades or guided tours

- **Unique Photo Opportunities:** Mist-covered roads, quiet village streets, mountain viewpoints

Practical Tips for a Seamless Winter Trip
Several small choices transformed my trip from good to effortless. Booking accommodation with heating and good insulation ensured comfort on cooler nights. Choosing centrally located bases reduced driving time and allowed for spontaneous exploration. I also built flexibility into my itinerary, allowing weather to guide my days rather than resisting it.

Winter rewards preparation but punishes rigidity. By planning thoughtfully and remaining adaptable, I experienced Madeira as it is meant to be enjoyed—without stress, without rush, and with room for discovery.

- **Suggested Travel Dates:** Flexible winter scheduling

- **Average Daily Planning Buffer:** €10–€20 for spontaneous activities

- **Unique Photo Opportunities:** Unplanned discoveries, changing skies, moments of stillness

Beginning Your Journey with Confidence

Planning a winter escape to Madeira does not require complexity, only intention. Once logistics are in place, the island takes over, offering clarity and calm. My experience taught me that preparation is not about control, but about creating space—space to walk, to observe, and to enjoy Madeira's quiet generosity. With these essentials handled, you are free to focus on what truly matters: experiencing the island fully, one winter day at a time.

Chapter 4: Where to Stay — Cozy Retreats to Oceanfront Luxury

Choosing the Right Base for a Winter Stay

Deciding where to stay in Madeira shaped my entire experience of the island. Because winter travel here is less frantic, the choice of base becomes less about proximity to attractions and more about atmosphere. I learned quickly that Madeira rewards travelers who choose a location aligned with their pace and interests. Whether I wanted easy access to cafés and museums or quiet evenings with ocean views, the island offered a place that felt right.

Winter made this decision easier. Availability was high, prices were reasonable, and I had the freedom to prioritize comfort and setting over urgency. Understanding the island's layout—coastal hubs, hillside retreats, and rural villages—helped me create a stay that felt balanced rather than fragmented.

- **Suggested Travel Dates:** December to February

- **Average Nightly Costs:** €70–€150 depending on location and style

- **Unique Photo Opportunities:** Balconies overlooking the Atlantic, hillside sunsets, early morning views from quiet neighborhoods

Funchal: Convenience, Culture, and Coastal Views

Funchal quickly became my anchor on the island. As Madeira's capital, it offers walkability, cultural depth, and reliable transport connections. Staying here in winter felt surprisingly calm. Cruise traffic was minimal, streets were relaxed, and evenings unfolded slowly. I could walk to markets, museums, and restaurants without planning, which made daily life feel intuitive.

Accommodation options in Funchal range widely—from modern hotels along the seafront to small guesthouses tucked into residential streets. I found mid-range hotels particularly good value in winter, often offering ocean views at prices that felt generous for the location.

- **Suggested Travel Dates:** January for quieter city life

- **Average Nightly Costs:** €80–€140

- **Unique Photo Opportunities:** Harbor reflections at dusk, tiled streets after rain, rooftop views over the bay

Câmara de Lobos and Surrounding Villages: Authentic and Unhurried

For travelers seeking something more local, Câmara de Lobos offers a compelling alternative. This fishing village, just outside Funchal, retains a strong sense of identity. I stayed nearby for a few nights and appreciated the slower mornings, sea-facing cafés, and absence of tourist pressure. Winter accentuates this calm, allowing daily routines to unfold naturally.

Boutique stays and apartments dominate this area. Many are family-run and designed with long stays in mind. Waking to the sound of the ocean and watching fishermen prepare their boats became part of my daily rhythm.

- **Suggested Travel Dates:** December to February

- **Average Nightly Costs:** €65–€110

- **Unique Photo Opportunities:** Fishing boats at dawn, cliffside villages, quiet harbors under winter light

North Coast Retreats: Nature at the Forefront

The north coast of Madeira, including places like São Vicente and Porto Moniz, feels more elemental. Weather here is slightly cooler and more dramatic, especially in winter, but that intensity is part of its appeal. I chose this region when I wanted proximity to nature rather than amenities. Mist, waves, and rugged terrain created an atmosphere that felt introspective and grounding.

Eco-lodges and rural guesthouses are common here, often set within lush landscapes. These stays suit travelers who plan to hike, photograph, or simply retreat. Winter makes the north coast particularly striking, though flexibility is essential when weather shifts.

- **Suggested Travel Dates:** November and February for dramatic scenery

- **Average Nightly Costs:** €60–€120

- **Unique Photo Opportunities:** Volcanic pools in rough seas, cloud-covered cliffs, forested valleys

Apartments and Long-Stay Comfort

Renting an apartment gave me the freedom to settle into daily life. Winter stays often come with discounted weekly or monthly rates, making apartments an excellent option for slow travelers and remote workers. Having a kitchen allowed me to shop at local markets and experience Madeira through routine rather than novelty.

Location mattered. I prioritized good insulation, heating, and natural light. Winter evenings can be cool, and comfort becomes essential. Well-chosen apartments enhanced the sense of temporary belonging that Madeira offers so readily.

- **Suggested Travel Dates:** January for extended stays

- **Average Nightly Costs:** €50–€100

- **Unique Photo Opportunities:** Interior details, morning light through windows, neighborhood scenes

Luxury and Wellness by the Sea

Madeira's reputation for refined hospitality is well-earned. Oceanfront resorts and historic hotels remain open year-round, and winter often brings quieter surroundings and attentive service. I spent a short stay at a wellness-focused hotel and found the experience deeply restorative. Heated pools, spa treatments, and sea views paired beautifully with winter's gentler pace.

Luxury in Madeira feels understated rather than showy. Properties emphasize comfort, tradition, and connection to landscape. Winter amplifies this sense of retreat, making indulgence feel purposeful rather than excessive.

- **Suggested Travel Dates:** December and January for serene luxury

- **Average Nightly Costs:** €150–€300

- **Unique Photo Opportunities:** Infinity pools against grey-blue seas, sunrise from private terraces, elegant interiors

Matching Your Stay to Your Travel Style

Ultimately, where you stay in Madeira should reflect how you wish to experience the island. Winter offers the rare opportunity to choose thoughtfully without compromise. City dwellers may prefer Funchal's accessibility, nature lovers the north coast, and slow travelers a well-located apartment. Each choice shapes daily rhythm, interactions, and perspective.

I learned that accommodation here is not just a place to sleep; it becomes part of the journey. By choosing a base that supports your intentions, winter in Madeira unfolds naturally—quiet, comfortable, and deeply rewarding.

Chapter 5: Getting Around Madeira

Understanding Madeira's Terrain Before You Move

Before choosing how to get around Madeira, I had to understand the island itself. Madeira is not flat, predictable, or forgiving of poor planning. Roads wind sharply along cliffs, climb steeply into the mountains, and drop suddenly toward the sea. Distances on the map can be misleading; what looks close may take time to reach. Winter adds another layer, with occasional fog at higher elevations and rain that changes road conditions quickly.

This geography shapes every transport decision. I learned that mobility here is less about speed and more about strategy—choosing the right mode of transport for the experience you want. Once I accepted that, navigating the island became far more enjoyable.

- **Suggested Travel Dates:** December to February for lighter traffic

- **Average Daily Transport Costs:** €10–€60 depending on mode

- **Unique Photo Opportunities:** Cliffside roads, mountain switchbacks, coastal viewpoints

Renting a Car: Freedom with Responsibility

Renting a car gave me the greatest flexibility, especially in winter when crowds are low and roads feel less pressured. I could stop at viewpoints spontaneously, adjust plans around weather, and explore rural areas without time constraints. Compact cars with good engines are ideal; Madeira's steep inclines demand power more than size.

Driving here requires confidence, not aggression. Narrow streets, sharp turns, and sudden elevation changes are common. Winter conditions can add fog in the mountains, making daytime driving preferable. I avoided night driving in unfamiliar areas and found that planning routes ahead of time reduced stress significantly.

- **Suggested Travel Dates:** January for easy parking and quieter roads

- **Average Daily Costs:** €30–€50 plus fuel

- **Unique Photo Opportunities:** Roadside viewpoints, quiet village roads, sunrise drives above the clouds

Public Transport: Practical but Limited

Madeira's bus network serves major towns well, particularly around Funchal. I relied on buses during my city stay and found them reliable and affordable. Winter schedules remain consistent, and buses are rarely crowded. However, routes become sparse in rural areas and mountainous regions, limiting access to some of the island's most scenic spots.

Public transport works best for travelers who plan to stay in Funchal or nearby towns and focus on urban exploration. For deeper island experiences, buses require patience and careful scheduling. I used them selectively, appreciating their simplicity while recognizing their limits.

- **Suggested Travel Dates:** December to February for comfortable rides

- **Average Daily Costs:** €5–€10

- **Unique Photo Opportunities:** Local life on bus routes, city streets from window views

Taxis and Ride Services: Convenient and Direct

Taxis proved invaluable for short distances, evening outings, or days when I wanted to avoid driving. They are widely available in Funchal and at major tourist areas. Prices are regulated, and drivers are knowledgeable, often sharing insights along the way. In winter, availability is rarely an issue, and wait times are short.

For travelers uncomfortable with Madeira's roads, taxis offer a stress-free alternative. I found them especially useful for airport transfers and late dinners, when driving unfamiliar routes in low light felt unnecessary.

- **Suggested Travel Dates:** All winter months
- **Average Ride Costs:** €10–€25 depending on distance
- **Unique Photo Opportunities:** City lights at night, harbor views from taxi routes

Guided Tours: Letting Someone Else Navigate

On days when weather was unpredictable or when I wanted context rather than control, guided tours were the right choice. Winter tours tend to be smaller and more flexible, allowing for personalized experiences. I joined a mountain tour that adjusted its route in response to fog, something I would not have managed alone.

Guided excursions remove logistical pressure and add depth through local knowledge. They are particularly valuable for first-time visitors or those interested in geology, wine, or wildlife. Winter enhances these tours by reducing crowds and fostering conversation.

- **Suggested Travel Dates:** February for wildlife and scenic tours

- **Average Tour Costs:** €45–€80

- **Unique Photo Opportunities:** Professionally timed viewpoints, wildlife sightings, group-free landscapes

Navigating the Mountains and Weather Wisely

Madeira's interior demands respect, especially in winter. Weather can change rapidly, and visibility may drop without warning. I learned to check forecasts each morning and remain flexible. When conditions were unclear, I postponed mountain drives or chose coastal alternatives.

Tunnel networks make travel easier, but reliance on GPS alone can be misleading. I cross-checked routes and allowed extra time. These habits turned potential challenges into manageable variables rather than obstacles.

- **Suggested Travel Dates:** January and February for misty mountain scenes

- **Average Additional Costs:** €0–€20 for detours or alternative transport

- **Unique Photo Opportunities:** Fog-draped peaks, dramatic weather shifts, layered landscapes

Choosing the Best Way to Move for Your Style

There is no single correct way to get around Madeira. Winter makes every option more approachable, allowing you to mix methods according to mood and destination. I combined car rentals with buses, taxis, and tours, creating a rhythm that felt balanced and intuitive.

Understanding the island's terrain and respecting its pace transformed movement into part of the experience rather than a hurdle. In Madeira, the journey between places often holds as much meaning as the destinations themselves.

Chapter 6: Winter Experiences You Can't Miss

Walking the Levadas in Winter Light

Levada walks were the reason I fell in love with Madeira's winter landscape. These centuries-old irrigation channels trace the island's contours, leading walkers through laurel forests, valleys, and along cliffs where water, stone, and greenery coexist in quiet harmony. Winter is when these paths feel most alive. Seasonal rainfall feeds the channels, moss thickens along the walls, and the air carries a cool freshness that makes long walks comfortable.

I chose my routes carefully, favoring well-maintained levadas such as Levada do Rei and Levada dos Balcões during winter. These walks offered manageable terrain and breathtaking scenery without unnecessary risk. The absence of summer crowds allowed me to pause often, listen to running water, and photograph details that would otherwise go unnoticed.

- **Suggested Travel Dates:** December to February

- **Average Costs:** Free for self-guided walks; €40–€60 for guided hikes
- **Unique Photo Opportunities:** Moss-covered channels, winter greenery, cloud-filtered forest light

Whale Watching Along a Winter Coast

Winter brought me one of Madeira's most moving experiences: whale watching. The waters around the island are active year-round, but winter offers particularly strong sightings of larger species. Standing on the deck of a small boat, watching the ocean swell beneath grey-blue skies, I felt the scale of the Atlantic in a way land never conveys.

Tours depart primarily from Funchal and Câmara de Lobos. Winter groups are smaller, which means clearer views and more attentive guides. I found the experience respectful and informative, with emphasis placed on observation rather than pursuit. Seeing a whale surface briefly before disappearing into deep water remains one of the most humbling moments of my trip.

- **Suggested Travel Dates:** February and early March

- **Average Costs:** €50–€70 per tour

- **Unique Photo Opportunities:** Whales breaking the surface, open-sea horizons, boats framed against winter skies

Cable Cars: Aerial Perspectives Without the Crowds

Taking the cable car from Funchal to Monte offered a different understanding of the island's verticality. Winter reduced wait times significantly, allowing for an unhurried ascent above the city. From the cabin, terracotta roofs gave way to gardens and hillsides, with the Atlantic stretching endlessly beyond.

At the top, cooler temperatures made walking through Monte's gardens pleasant rather than exhausting. The experience felt contemplative rather than touristic. Cable cars in winter are not about spectacle; they are about perspective.

- **Suggested Travel Dates:** January for minimal queues

- **Average Costs:** €12–€18 one way

- **Unique Photo Opportunities:** Aerial views of Funchal, layered hillsides, winter light over the harbor

Natural Pools and Winter Seas

Visiting Madeira's natural pools in winter is not about swimming in the traditional sense. At Porto Moniz, I stood watching waves surge and spill into volcanic basins, a dramatic reminder of the island's raw nature. On calmer days, I ventured into the water briefly, invigorated by the contrast between sea and air.

Winter seas transform these pools into living sculptures. Even without entering the water, the experience felt complete. The sound of waves, the scent of salt, and the sight of water crashing against black volcanic stone created an atmosphere that lingered long after I left.

- **Suggested Travel Dates:** November to February for dramatic seas

- **Average Costs:** €3–€5 entry where applicable

- **Unique Photo Opportunities:** Waves exploding over pools, moody coastlines, mist rising from the sea

Spas and Thermal Comfort

After days of walking and exploring, Madeira's spa culture offered welcome restoration. Winter made these experiences especially meaningful. Heated pools, saunas, and massage treatments contrasted beautifully with the cooler air outside. I chose spas connected to hotels overlooking the sea, where relaxation felt integrated with landscape.

These spaces are not indulgent escapes but extensions of Madeira's emphasis on balance and well-being. Winter quiet enhances the sense of retreat, allowing time to rest without distraction.

- **Suggested Travel Dates:** December to January

- **Average Costs:** €30–€80 depending on treatment

- **Unique Photo Opportunities:** Steam against ocean views, minimalist spa interiors, sunset from poolside

Christmas Markets and Festive Traditions

December in Madeira surprised me with its warmth—both literal and cultural. Christmas markets filled Funchal with lights, music, and the scent of traditional foods. Unlike larger European cities, these markets felt intimate and locally focused. Families gathered, musicians played, and conversations flowed easily.

I spent evenings wandering through decorated streets, sampling seasonal treats and observing traditions that blend Portuguese heritage with island character. The festive season here is not overwhelming; it is inviting.

- **Suggested Travel Dates:** Early to mid-December

- **Average Costs:** €10–€20 for food and souvenirs

- **Unique Photo Opportunities:** Illuminated streets, market details, evening harbor lights

Seasonal Outdoor Adventures

Winter in Madeira still invites adventure. I explored coastal walks, moderate hikes, and viewpoints without the fatigue of summer heat. Activities like paragliding, canyoning, and cycling remain available, though winter encourages careful planning and flexibility. I chose days with stable weather and always prioritized safety over ambition.

The reward was clarity—both literal and mental. Winter landscapes feel sharper, more expressive, and deeply satisfying. Adventure here is not about extremes, but about connection.

- **Suggested Travel Dates:** January and February for balanced conditions

- **Average Costs:** €40–€90 depending on activity

- **Unique Photo Opportunities:** Cliffside views, motion-filled landscapes, solitary outdoor moments

Experiencing Madeira at Its Most Authentic

Winter experiences in Madeira share a common thread: intimacy. Whether walking a levada, watching whales, or standing quietly at a viewpoint, the island feels open and generous. These moments do not demand attention; they reward it.

This season allows Madeira to reveal itself slowly, offering experiences that feel personal rather than programmed. For travelers willing to engage fully, winter delivers the island in its most honest form—rich, reflective, and unforgettable.

Chapter 7: Exploring Funchal and Beyond

Funchal: The Island's Living Heart

Funchal became my starting point and, in many ways, my anchor. As Madeira's capital, it blends everyday life with history and quiet elegance. Winter softened the city's edges. Streets felt breathable, cafés lingered over conversations, and the harbor reflected muted skies rather than cruise ships. I spent mornings walking without direction, letting tiled sidewalks and hillside views guide me.

Neighborhoods revealed themselves gradually. The Old Town, with its painted doors and stone alleys, felt intimate rather than performative in winter. I lingered at the farmers' market, not just to photograph produce but to observe the rhythm of trade. Funchal rewards attention—its charm lies in details rather than landmarks.

- **Suggested Travel Dates:** January for unhurried exploration

- **Average Daily Costs:** €25–€40 for food and local transport

- **Unique Photo Opportunities:** Harbor reflections, tiled streets after rain, market details

Monte and the Hills Above the City

Rising above Funchal, Monte offers a change in perspective and pace. I reached it by cable car, watching the city recede as gardens and hills took over. Winter temperatures made walking through Monte's botanical spaces comfortable, allowing time to absorb the quiet beauty of the surroundings.

The area carries a sense of retreat. Historic villas, churchyards, and viewpoints invite pause rather than movement. From here, Funchal feels distant, almost abstract. Monte is not a place to rush; it is a place to look down and reflect.

- **Suggested Travel Dates:** December to February

- **Average Costs:** €12–€18 for cable car; minimal costs on foot

- **Unique Photo Opportunities:** Aerial city views, misty gardens, layered hillside perspectives

Câmara de Lobos and Coastal Villages

Just west of Funchal, Câmara de Lobos offered one of my most authentic coastal experiences. This fishing village retains a working identity, especially visible in winter when tourism recedes. Boats bob quietly in the harbor, nets dry along the shore, and cafés serve locals first.

Exploring nearby coastal villages revealed a pattern: small centers, strong community ties, and landscapes shaped by both sea and slope. Winter made these places approachable, allowing me to observe rather than intrude. The ocean here feels closer, more present.

- **Suggested Travel Dates:** January and February

- **Average Daily Costs:** €15–€30

- **Unique Photo Opportunities:** Fishing boats at dawn, coastal cliffs, village harbors under winter light

The North Coast: Dramatic and Untamed

The north coast felt like a different island altogether. Places like São Vicente and Seixal introduced me to Madeira's raw side—steeper cliffs, rougher seas, and weather that shifts quickly. Winter amplified this drama, wrapping mountains in mist and deepening the color of the ocean.
Despite the intensity, these towns remain welcoming. I found quiet cafés, small museums, and walking paths that encouraged observation. The north coast demands respect and rewards

patience. It is a place for travelers drawn to atmosphere rather than convenience.

- **Suggested Travel Dates:** November and February

- **Average Daily Costs:** €20–€35

- **Unique Photo Opportunities:** Wave-swept coastlines, fog-draped villages, volcanic beaches

Mountain Escapes and High-Altitude Views

Venturing into Madeira's interior changed my understanding of the island. The mountains create their own weather, and winter accentuates this separation. I drove up to Pico do Arieiro on a clear morning and found myself above the clouds, surrounded by silence and space.

High-altitude areas are not about constant movement. Short walks, viewpoints, and moments of stillness define the experience. Winter's cooler air and shifting light make these escapes especially compelling, though flexibility remains essential.

- **Suggested Travel Dates:** January for cloud inversions

- **Average Costs:** €0–€10 for self-guided exploration

- **Unique Photo Opportunities:** Sea of clouds, rugged peaks, sunrise over the mountains

Hidden Corners and Lesser-Known Paths

Some of my most memorable moments came from places I had not planned to visit. Small villages, overlooked viewpoints, and side roads revealed scenes untouched by expectation. Winter makes these discoveries easier; with fewer distractions, the island invites curiosity.

I learned to trust instinct—turning down unfamiliar roads, stopping when something caught my eye. These choices led to conversations, views, and moments that felt entirely my own. Madeira's hidden corners are not secret; they simply require time.

- **Suggested Travel Dates:** Throughout winter for spontaneous exploration

- **Average Daily Costs:** €0–€15

- **Unique Photo Opportunities:** Unmarked viewpoints, everyday village life, fleeting winter light

Seeing the Island as a Whole

Exploring Funchal and beyond in winter allowed me to understand Madeira as a connected landscape rather than isolated highlights. City, coast, and mountains flow into one another, each influencing the next. Winter removes the noise, revealing continuity.

This chapter is not an itinerary but an invitation—to explore with intention, to look beyond the obvious, and to allow the island's diversity to unfold gradually. Madeira reveals its depth to those willing to move slowly, especially when winter sets the tone.

Chapter 8: Food, Wine, and Local Flavors

Eating Madeira in Winter: A Seasonal Perspective

Winter changed how I ate in Madeira. Cooler evenings invited slower meals, heartier plates, and longer conversations at the table. Unlike summer, when dining often feels rushed between activities, winter encourages sitting down with intention. Restaurants feel more local, menus lean toward comfort, and seasonal ingredients quietly take center stage.

What struck me most was how deeply food here is tied to place. Meals are not constructed for spectacle; they are built from habit, tradition, and availability. Eating well in Madeira during winter is less about chasing trends and more about understanding rhythm.

- **Suggested Travel Dates:** December to February

- **Average Meal Costs:** €10–€18 for local eateries, €25–€40 for refined dining

- **Unique Photo Opportunities:** Steaming dishes on wooden tables, candlelit interiors, rain-dimmed street cafés

Traditional Madeiran Dishes Worth Sitting Down For

I began my culinary exploration with dishes that locals order without hesitation. Espetada—chunks of beef grilled on bay leaf skewers—was my introduction to Madeira's unapologetic approach to flavor. Served simply with fried cornmeal and salad, it tasted elemental and honest.

Then there was espada com banana, a pairing that initially sounded unlikely but quickly made sense. The mild black scabbardfish balances beautifully with caramelized banana, especially comforting on winter evenings. Soups, particularly wheat-based caldo and vegetable-rich broths, appeared frequently and were always deeply satisfying.

- **Suggested Travel Dates:** January for full seasonal menus

- **Average Costs:** €12–€20 per traditional dish

- **Unique Photo Opportunities:** Hanging espetada skewers, rustic table settings, steam rising from bowls

Winter Comfort Foods and Home-Style Cooking
Winter in Madeira brings out dishes meant to sustain rather than impress. I noticed more slow-cooked meats, heavier sauces, and

generous portions. These meals felt like extensions of home kitchens rather than restaurant creations.

I gravitated toward small, family-run places where menus were short and explanations came willingly. Bread arrived warm, often homemade, and butter or garlic spreads followed without request. Desserts leaned toward puddings and custards rather than pastries, offering warmth rather than sweetness alone.

- **Suggested Travel Dates:** December through February
- **Average Costs:** €8–€15 for hearty plates
- **Unique Photo Opportunities:** Earthenware dishes, communal tables, handwritten menus

Poncha Culture: More Than a Drink
Poncha is not merely consumed in Madeira; it is shared. I learned quickly that ordering poncha invites conversation. Made from aguardente de cana, honey, and citrus, it varies subtly from bar to bar. Winter versions often feel stronger, meant to warm rather than refresh.

Standing at wooden counters in small taverns, I watched bartenders mix drinks by feel rather than measure. Locals sipped slowly, often accompanied by nuts or conversation rather than music. It became clear that poncha is less about alcohol and more about presence.

- **Suggested Travel Dates:** Evenings year-round, especially winter

- **Average Costs:** €2–€4 per glass

- **Unique Photo Opportunities:** Wooden mixing tools, citrus-stained counters, intimate bar scenes

Madeira Wine: Tasting History in a Glass
Wine tasting in winter felt appropriate—reflective and unrushed. Madeira wine carries centuries of history, and tasting it where it originates adds depth to every sip. I explored several lodges in Funchal, learning how oxidation and aging define the wine's character.

Each style told a different story, from dry Sercial to rich Malvasia. Winter allowed time to appreciate nuance without the distraction of crowds. Tastings felt educational rather than promotional, grounding the experience in tradition.

- **Suggested Travel Dates:** January and February

- **Average Costs:** €10–€20 for guided tastings

- **Unique Photo Opportunities:** Barrel-lined cellars, amber wine glasses, historic tasting rooms

Bakeries and Sweet Traditions

Morning rituals in Madeira often begin at bakeries, and winter made these visits especially comforting. I followed locals rather than reviews, stepping into unassuming shops where queues formed early. Bolo do caco, still warm and brushed with garlic butter, became my preferred breakfast.

Sweet treats leaned toward understated flavors—molasses cakes, custards, and nut-based pastries. These were not desserts designed for display, but for consumption. Sitting with coffee while rain tapped against windows became one of my most repeated pleasures.

- **Suggested Travel Dates:** Any winter morning

- **Average Costs:** €1–€4 per item

- **Unique Photo Opportunities**: Fresh bread trays, bakery counters, morning light through shop windows

Where Locals Eat: Reading the Room

Finding where locals eat required observation more than research. Places filled with conversation rather than décor proved reliable.

Menus posted outside in Portuguese, limited opening hours, and handwritten specials often signaled authenticity.

I noticed that lunchtime drew larger crowds than dinner, with workers returning home early in winter evenings. Following these patterns led me to meals that felt integrated into daily life rather than curated for visitors.

- **Suggested Travel Dates:** Weekdays for genuine atmosphere

- **Average Costs:** €9–€14 for set lunches

- **Unique Photo Opportunities:** Busy lunchrooms, chalkboard menus, everyday dining rituals

Markets and Ingredients: Understanding the Source
Visiting local markets helped contextualize everything I ate. Winter produce reflected resilience—root vegetables, citrus, greens. Fish stalls displayed what the sea allowed rather than abundance. Conversations with vendors added dimension, revealing how weather shapes availability.

Markets are not just places to shop; they are places to listen. Observing these exchanges helped me appreciate meals not as isolated experiences but as outcomes of landscape and season.

- **Suggested Travel Dates:** Morning visits year-round

- **Average Costs:** €5–€15 for snacks and produce

- **Unique Photo Opportunities:** Produce textures, fish displays, vendor interactions

Tasting Madeira Slowly

Food in Madeira taught me patience. Winter reinforces this lesson, encouraging meals that unfold rather than conclude quickly. I stopped chasing recommendations and began trusting repetition—returning to places that felt right.

This chapter is not a checklist but a lens. Eating here is about aligning with season, listening to locals, and allowing flavors to reveal themselves gradually. Madeira's culinary identity does not shout; it speaks quietly, rewarding those willing to stay at the table a little longer.

Chapter 9: Madeira for Every Type of Traveler

Traveling Solo: Freedom, Safety, and Self-Discovery

Traveling alone in Madeira felt effortless in a way that few destinations manage. From the moment I arrived, I noticed how naturally solo travelers blend into daily life here. Cafés welcome lingering, trails feel secure, and conversations unfold easily, even without invitation. Winter, in particular, brings a calm that suits introspection and unhurried exploration.

I spent mornings walking levadas alone, often encountering the same faces along the paths, which created an unspoken sense of community. Public transport and taxis felt reliable, and locals were quick to offer guidance when asked. Madeira's safety record and relaxed rhythm made solo travel feel less like isolation and more like quiet independence.

- **Suggested Travel Dates:** January to early March

- **Average Daily Costs:** €55–€80

- **Unique Photo Opportunities:** Misty mountain trails, solitary café tables, cliffside viewpoints

Couples and Romantic Escapes

Madeira reveals its romantic side slowly. Winter evenings encourage candlelit dinners, while cooler temperatures make walking hand in hand through historic streets comfortable rather than hurried. I noticed couples lingering at viewpoints long after sunset, wrapped in shared silence rather than spectacle.

Oceanfront hotels and hillside retreats create natural intimacy, especially when fog drifts in from the sea. Cable car rides over Funchal, wine tastings in old cellars, and spa afternoons all feel designed for two, without being overly staged.

- **Suggested Travel Dates:** December to February

- **Average Daily Costs:** €120–€200 per couple

- **Unique Photo Opportunities:** Sunset terraces, vineyard views, rain-washed streets

Honeymooners Seeking Quiet Luxury

For honeymooners, Madeira offers understated indulgence. This is not a destination of grand gestures but of thoughtful details. I observed how resorts emphasize privacy over performance, offering private pools, ocean-facing balconies, and attentive service without intrusion.

Winter amplifies this sense of exclusivity. Fewer visitors mean more personalized experiences—private wine tastings, quiet spa circuits, and uninterrupted dinners. The island's landscapes do much of the emotional work, creating a backdrop that feels intimate rather than overwhelming.

- **Suggested Travel Dates:** January or February

- **Average Daily Costs:** €220–€350

- **Unique Photo Opportunities:** Cliffside infinity pools, fog-draped mornings, candlelit dinners

Families Traveling with Children
Traveling with children in Madeira requires thoughtful pacing, and winter makes that easier. Cooler weather reduces fatigue, and many activities naturally suit younger travelers. I noticed families enjoying botanical gardens, cable cars, and natural pools without the pressure of extreme heat.

Accommodations often provide family rooms or apartments, making longer stays comfortable. Restaurants are generally welcoming, and portions are generous enough for sharing. Winter festivals and holiday decorations add an extra layer of excitement for children, especially in December.

- **Suggested Travel Dates:** December holidays or February

- **Average Daily Costs:** €100–€160

- **Unique Photo Opportunities:** Cable car views, festive streets, natural pool splashes

Digital Nomads and Remote Workers

As someone who values both productivity and environment, I found Madeira particularly appealing for remote work. Winter brings quieter cafés, stable internet, and a rhythm that supports focus. Funchal, especially, offers coworking spaces and apartments designed for longer stays.

Mornings were ideal for work, afternoons for walks, and evenings for simple meals. The cost of living remains reasonable compared to other European islands, and the scenery provides daily inspiration without distraction.

- **Suggested Travel Dates:** November to March
- **Average Monthly Costs:** €1,200–€1,800

- **Unique Photo Opportunities:** Laptop setups with ocean views, café workspaces, sunset breaks

Retirees and Leisure Travelers

Madeira has long attracted retirees, and winter showcases why. The climate remains gentle, healthcare is accessible, and daily life unfolds at a comfortable pace. I noticed many long-term visitors who return annually, drawn by routine rather than novelty.

Walking paths, gardens, and cultural centers provide daily structure without physical strain. Social life appears quietly vibrant, centered around cafés, markets, and community events rather than nightlife.

- **Suggested Travel Dates:** January to March

- **Average Daily Costs:** €70–€110

- **Unique Photo Opportunities:** Garden benches, seaside promenades, morning markets

Slow Travelers and Long-Stay Visitors

Madeira rewards those who stay longer. Winter invites repetition—returning to the same bakery, trail, or viewpoint until it feels familiar. I experienced how staying put deepens understanding, transforming sightseeing into participation.

Rental apartments offer better value for extended stays, and public transport becomes intuitive over time. Slow travel here feels natural, as the island's size encourages exploration without urgency.

- **Suggested Travel Dates:** January through March

- **Average Weekly Costs:** €400–€700

- **Unique Photo Opportunities:** Daily routines, familiar faces, changing light over known landscapes

Finding Your Place in Madeira
What Madeira offers is not a single experience but a framework adaptable to many needs. Whether seeking solitude, connection, rest, or renewal, the island adjusts without losing its identity. Winter strips away excess, revealing a destination that meets travelers where they are.

This flexibility is Madeira's quiet strength. It does not demand a specific way of visiting. Instead, it allows each traveler to shape the journey according to their rhythm, making every stay feel personal rather than prescribed.

Chapter 10: Suggested Winter Itineraries

How I Approach Winter Itineraries in Madeira

When I travel to Madeira in winter, I plan with gentleness in mind. The island reveals itself best when days are not overfilled. Weather shifts subtly, light lingers differently on the mountains, and some of the most memorable moments happen between destinations rather than at them. These itineraries are shaped by my own experiences—days that balanced exploration with rest, movement with stillness. Each route allows flexibility while ensuring you experience Madeira's landscapes, culture, and seasonal character without fatigue.

A 3-Day Winter Escape: First Impressions and Coastal Calm

This short itinerary suits travelers arriving for a long weekend or those testing the waters before committing to a longer stay. I designed it to offer a gentle introduction without rushing the experience.

Day 1: Arrival and Funchal at Leisure

After arriving at Cristiano Ronaldo International Airport, I always recommend settling into your accommodation before venturing out. Winter flights tend to be smoother and less crowded, making arrival surprisingly relaxed.

Spend the afternoon exploring Funchal's old town. I like to begin at Rua de Santa Maria, where painted doors add color to quiet winter streets. Dinner near the harbor feels especially peaceful this time of year.

- **Suggested Travel Dates:** December to February

- **Average Daily Cost:** €70–€120

- **Unique Photo Opportunities:** Painted doors, harbor reflections at dusk

Day 2: Monte and Botanical Beauty

Mornings in winter feel crisp but comfortable. I take the cable car up to Monte, enjoying views over the city as clouds drift past the hills. The Monte Palace Tropical Garden remains lush year-round, offering warmth through greenery alone.

If weather permits, the traditional toboggan ride adds a playful touch. The afternoon is ideal for café hopping or visiting a small museum before an early evening.

- **Average Daily Cost:** €80–€130

- **Unique Photo Opportunities:** Garden terraces, cable car vistas

Day 3: Câmara de Lobos and Departure
Before leaving, I head west to Câmara de Lobos. The fishing village feels quieter in winter, allowing time to appreciate its rhythms. A simple seafood lunch here feels like a farewell ritual.

- **Average Daily Cost:** €60–€100

- **Unique Photo Opportunities:** Colorful boats, coastal cliffs

A 5-Day Winter Journey: Nature, Culture, and Balance
This itinerary suits travelers who want a deeper understanding of Madeira without feeling overwhelmed. Five days allow for both city life and nature immersion.

Days 1–2: Funchal and Surroundings

Begin as in the 3-day itinerary, but allow extra time for markets, wine tasting, and museums. Winter mornings are perfect for visiting Mercado dos Lavradores without crowds.

- **Suggested Travel Dates:** January to early March

- **Average Daily Cost:** €80–€140

- **Unique Photo Opportunities:** Market stalls, wine cellars

Day 3: Levada Walks and Forest Landscapes

One of my favorite winter experiences is walking a levada under light mist. Trails like Levada do Caldeirão Verde feel almost otherworldly in winter light. Guided tours are helpful for navigation and safety.

- **Average Daily Cost:** €90–€150

- **Unique Photo Opportunities:** Water channels, moss-covered tunnels

Day 4: Northern Coast and Natural Pools

The north coast feels dramatic year-round, but winter waves add texture to the landscape. Porto Moniz's natural pools remain accessible on calm days, offering a striking contrast to the cooler air.

- **Average Daily Cost:** €80–€130

- **Unique Photo Opportunities:** Lava pools, crashing waves

Day 5: Free Exploration and Departure
Use the final day for unplanned wandering. I often revisit a favorite café or viewpoint before leaving.

- **Average Daily Cost:** €60–€100

- **Unique Photo Opportunities:** Familiar streets in changing light

A 7-Day Winter Immersion: Slow Travel and Depth

Seven days allow Madeira to unfold gradually. This itinerary is ideal for nature lovers and first-time visitors who value rhythm over speed.

Days 1–3: Funchal and Cultural Exploration
Take time to settle in. Visit neighborhoods, attend a winter concert, or explore smaller galleries. The slower pace reveals daily life beyond tourism.

- **Suggested Travel Dates:** January through March

- **Average Daily Cost:** €80–€150

- **Unique Photo Opportunities:** Neighborhood details, evening lights

Days 4–5: Mountains and Eastern Madeira

Driving through the interior reveals changing climates within minutes. Pico do Arieiro often sits above clouds, creating unforgettable views. Winter mornings are best for visibility.

- **Average Daily Cost:** €100–€180

- **Unique Photo Opportunities:** Cloud inversions, mountain ridges

Day 6: Southern Coast and Relaxation

Spend a day unwinding. Spas, coastal walks, or a long lunch overlooking the ocean provide balance after active days.

- **Average Daily Cost:** €90–€160

- **Unique Photo Opportunities:** Ocean terraces, sunset skies

Day 7: Reflection and Farewell

I reserve the final day for reflection—walking familiar paths and absorbing the quiet before departure. Madeira leaves an impression that lingers long after leaving.

- **Average Daily Cost:** €60–€100

- **Unique Photo Opportunities:** Early morning streets, final viewpoints

Adapting These Itineraries to Your Style

These winter itineraries are guides, not rules. Madeira encourages flexibility. Weather may shift plans, but often leads to unexpected discoveries. By allowing space in your schedule, you experience the island as it presents itself—unfiltered, calm, and deeply rewarding.

Conclusion: Leaving Madeira, Carrying the Warmth With You

The Quiet Weight of Departure

Leaving Madeira never felt like an ending to me; it felt more like a pause. On my final morning, as I watched the light stretch slowly across the Atlantic, I understood why this island lingers in memory. Winter strips travel of excess, and Madeira wears the season gracefully. There is no urgency here, no demand to rush. Departure arrives gently, almost reluctantly, as if the island itself resists goodbyes.

- **Suggested Travel Dates for Farewell Moments:** Late January to early March

- **Average Final-Day Costs:** €40–€70

- **Unique Photo Opportunities:** Early morning harbor light, departing ferries

What Madeira Teaches You About Time

One of Madeira's quiet lessons is its relationship with time. Winter days unfold without spectacle, allowing travelers to notice subtleties—how clouds settle into valleys, how conversations linger over coffee, how landscapes change by the hour rather than the minute. I found myself moving slower without effort, adapting to a rhythm that felt both natural and restorative.

This recalibration stayed with me long after leaving. Madeira does not ask for productivity or performance; it invites presence. That shift is perhaps the island's greatest gift.

- **Suggested Travel Dates:** Entire winter season

- **Average Daily Costs During Reflection Days:** €50–€90

- **Unique Photo Opportunities:** Shifting cloud patterns, empty promenades

Landscapes That Resurface in Memory
Long after the journey ended, certain images returned unprompted. A levada path disappearing into fog. A cliff edge where land met sea without ceremony. A quiet café where the same faces appeared each morning. Madeira's landscapes do not overwhelm; they settle in quietly, resurfacing when least expected.

Winter light softens everything. It turns ordinary scenes into lasting impressions. These visuals become anchors—reminders of calm when life elsewhere accelerates.

- **Suggested Travel Dates:** January to February

- **Average Costs for Scenic Days:** €30–€60

- **Unique Photo Opportunities:** Misty trails, subdued coastal tones

Human Connections That Endure

While Madeira's scenery is unforgettable, its people shape the experience just as deeply. Conversations were unforced, hospitality understated. Locals shared stories without performance, offering insight through everyday interactions rather than rehearsed narratives.

These exchanges grounded the journey. They reminded me that travel is not only about place, but about the human texture that defines it.

- **Suggested Travel Dates:** Winter months with fewer crowds

- **Average Daily Costs:** €20–€40 for local dining

- **Unique Photo Opportunities:** Market exchanges, café interiors

Carrying Madeira Home
What I carried home from Madeira was not a checklist of attractions but a way of being. Winter on the island showed me how travel can restore rather than exhaust. It reinforced the value of stillness, of choosing depth over breadth, of letting places reveal themselves gradually.

Madeira's warmth is not defined by temperature alone. It exists in light, landscape, and the ease of daily life. Long after winter fades, that warmth remains—quiet, steady, and deeply personal.

- **Suggested Travel Dates for Lasting Impact:** January through March

- **Average Trip Cost (Overall):** €900–€1,500

- **Unique Photo Opportunities:** Final glances, layered memories

A Journey That Continues
Even now, Madeira returns in small ways—in how I walk, how I pause, how I listen. That is the mark of a place that offers more than escape. It offers perspective. Winter may end, but the island's influence does not. It travels with you, shaping how you move through the world long after the journey concludes.

Appendix

Emergency Numbers & Useful Contacts

Knowing who to call in unfamiliar territory brings peace of mind, especially in winter when weather can change plans quickly. During my time in Madeira, I found emergency services reliable and well-coordinated. Portugal uses a centralized emergency number, making access straightforward even for visitors.

- Emergency Services (Police, Fire, Ambulance): 112

- Police (PSP): Available in Funchal and major towns

- Hospital Dr. Nélio Mendonça (Funchal): Main public hospital on the island

- Pharmacies: Clearly marked with green crosses; many operate rotating night shifts

- Tourist Information Centers: Located in Funchal, airport, and key towns

I kept these details saved on my phone and written in my travel notebook—simple preparation that allowed me to explore with confidence.

- **Suggested Travel Dates:** Year-round

- **Average Cost:** Free

- **Unique Photo Opportunities:** Historic police buildings, town signage

Seasonal Events & Festivals

Winter in Madeira is rich with cultural rhythm. Events feel rooted in community rather than spectacle, and visitors are welcomed naturally.

- **Christmas and New Year Celebrations (December):** Funchal's lights and fireworks are among Europe's most impressive.

- **Janeiras (January):** Traditional singing groups move through villages, celebrating the new year.

- **Carnival (February):** Colorful parades blend humor, music, and local flair.

I planned my visits around these dates to experience Madeira at its most expressive, yet never overwhelming.

- **Suggested Travel Dates:** December to February

- **Average Cost:** €0–€30

- **Unique Photo Opportunities:** Festive lights, street performances

Basic Portuguese Phrases

While many Madeirans speak English, learning a few Portuguese phrases transformed my interactions. Locals responded warmly, often switching languages with a smile.

Bom dia: Good morning

Boa tarde: Good afternoon

Boa noite: Good evening

Por favor: Please

Obrigado/Obrigada: Thank you (male/female speaker)

Desculpe: Excuse me / Sorry

Quanto custa?: How much does it cost?

These simple words opened conversations and signaled respect.

- **Suggested Travel Dates:** Anytime

- **Average Cost:** Free

- **Unique Photo Opportunities:** Handwritten menus, street signs

Packing Checklist for Winter

Winter packing for Madeira is about layers rather than bulk. I learned quickly that weather can shift between coastal warmth and mountain chill within an hour.

Essentials I Always Carry:

- Lightweight waterproof jacket

- Comfortable walking shoes with grip

- Layered clothing (long sleeves, light sweaters)

- Scarf or light shawl

- Daypack for walks

- Reusable water bottle

Packing smart allowed flexibility without overloading my luggage.

- **Suggested Travel Dates:** November to March
- **Average Cost:** €0–€150 depending on gear
- **Unique Photo Opportunities:** Layered outfits against scenic backdrops

Maps & Planning Resources

While digital maps are reliable, I found value in combining them with physical references.

- **Offline Maps:** Useful in mountain areas
- **Tourist Office Maps:** Highlight walking paths and viewpoints
- **Local Bus Schedules:** Available online and at terminals

Having multiple planning tools ensured smooth navigation, especially on levada walks.

- **Suggested Travel Dates:** Year-round

- **Average Cost:** Free

- **Unique Photo Opportunities:** Folded maps, trail markers

Travel Tips at a Glance

- Over time, small habits improved my experience significantly.

- Start days early for clearer mountain views

- Check weather by region, not just city forecasts

- Allow buffer time for driving narrow roads
- Embrace flexibility—plans often improve when adjusted

These insights came from experience rather than guides, shaping a journey that felt intuitive rather than forced.

- **Suggested Travel Dates:** Winter season

- **Average Cost:** Free

- **Unique Photo Opportunities:** Morning light, spontaneous moments

Final Notes for Thoughtful Travel

This appendix exists to support exploration, not constrain it. Madeira rewards preparation but values openness. By balancing structure with curiosity, winter travel here becomes less about logistics and more about presence. With these resources at hand, the island opens itself gently—ready to be experienced, not rushed.

Printed in Dunstable, United Kingdom